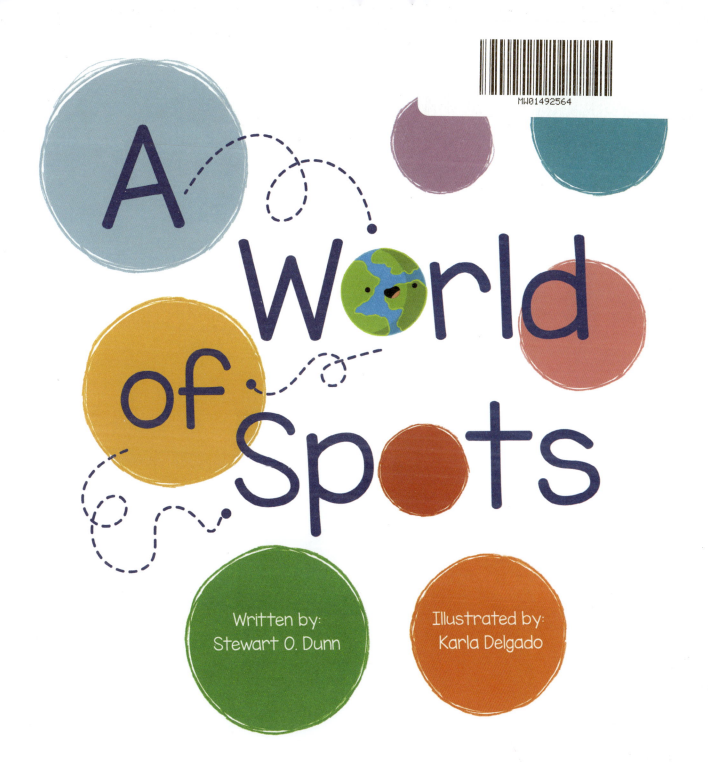

A World of Spots

Written by:
Stewart O. Dunn

Illustrated by:
Karla Delgado

Liam,
Never stop learning
because life never stops
teaching!
-♡- Stewart O. Dunn

Publisher
Stewart O. Dunn
www.stewartodunn.com

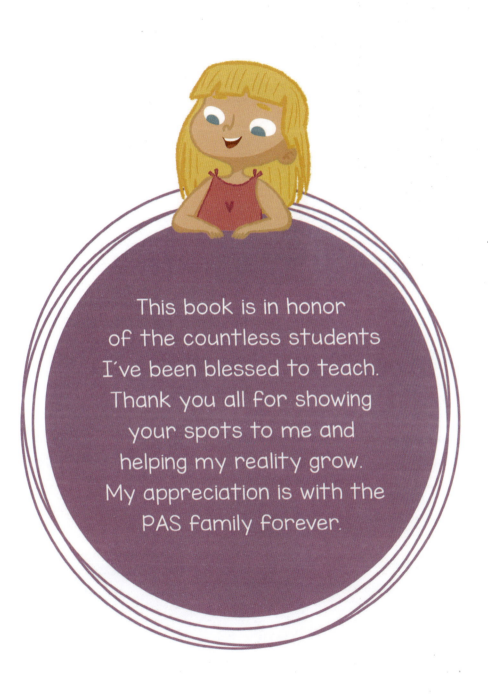

This book is in honor
of the countless students
I've been blessed to teach.
Thank you all for showing
your spots to me and
helping my reality grow.
My appreciation is with the
PAS family forever.

We all live life on the same spot in the universe.

On this spot, life is lived in many different ways.

you are here

We experience the world from the spot we are in.

We think, act, and respond to life based on what we learn in our spots.

These spots help us understand
ourselves and others.

Each spot colors our
world a little more.

Compare the spot from up high
and from down low.

Because the more spots you know,
the more your world grows.

Other times, we have different views from the same spot.

Since one spot can show us many things,
we choose what to focus on!

Study the spot from afar
and from up close.

Because the more spots you know,
the more your world grows.

Once in a while, we return to a spot
only to realize we've changed.

Decide when to hang on
and when to let go.

Because the more spots you know,
the more your world grows.

Not everyone will understand what we feel in our spots.

Remember, our emotions are not permanent. They come and go and change with each moment.

We spend more time in certain spots.

Whether you are sharing
a goodbye or a hello,

the more spots you know,
the more your world grows.

Our reactions and opinions change
the more we learn about a spot.

There is usually
more to a spot
than we can see.

Consider the spot from above
and from below.

Because the more spots you know,
the more your world grows.

We can ask to share in someone's spot.

And we can invite
others to visit
our spot.

Look up to the sky and admire the rainbow.

Because the more spots you know, the more your world grows.

You have your truth and I have mine. We don't need to experience every spot to live together peacefully.

All spots are special.
All spots add color.

Celebrate our connections
and what life has to show.

Our world is made more beautiful
with every spot we come to know!